AF504681

RECOGNITION OF TRADE UNIONS AND RIGHTS OF RECOGNIZED TRADE UNIONS

VOLUME 2, ISSUE 1 OF BRILLOPEDIA

KISLAY TARUN

Copyright © Kislay Tarun
All Rights Reserved.

ISBN 979-888569857-3

This book has been published with all efforts taken to make the material error-free after the consent of the author. However, the author and the publisher do not assume and hereby disclaim any liability to any party for any loss, damage, or disruption caused by errors or omissions, whether such errors or omissions result from negligence, accident, or any other cause.

While every effort has been made to avoid any mistake or omission, this publication is being sold on the condition and understanding that neither the author nor the publishers or printers would be liable in any manner to any person by reason of any mistake or omission in this publication or for any action taken or omitted to be taken or advice rendered or accepted on the basis of this work. For any defect in printing or binding the publishers will be liable only to replace the defective copy by another copy of this work then available.

Contents

Preface

"Start writing, no matter what. The water does not flow until the faucet is turned on".

-Louis L'Amour

Hundreds of students and professors are contributing their work to Brillopedia, we are here to provide ample information about Law and Contemporary issues. Our aim is to provide a platform for today's generation to express their views and ideas on law and contemporary law.

Publication

This research paper is published in volume 2, Issue 1 of Brillopedia

• vii •

Author

Kislay Tarun

CHAPTER ONE

Background of the study/ Abstract

When one talks about the economy of a country, the two elements which hit the mind are "Trade" and "Industry." The industrial organizations are a giant hall of trade aspects which consists of certain unions formed by the labors, and one such major union is the "Trade Union." Any formed union acts and operates as an organization, and it is a requirement for that organization to be recognized in its sector. The same is the case with the recognition of the Trade Unions and once these unions get recognized, certain rights get vested in them and they are free to enjoy those rights without interruptions. The Labor and Industrial Laws are responsible for the recognition of these unions and the protection of their rights after recognition. But the two major questions which arise here is- Are these Trade Unions fairly and easily recognized in the Industrial Sector and if so, are they freely allowed to exercise their conferred rights and privileges relating to trade and industrial operations.

The core objective of this Research Paper is to examine and analyze the challenges and perspectives in the procedure of recognition of Trade Unionsand the major Rights conferred in them and how freely and fairly their rights are accepted and respected in the Industrial and Trade sector for the betterment of the economy and the respectful operation of labors and their integrity.

In recent times, it has been noticed that the Trade Unions and Labors are opting for methods such as Strikes and Lockouts to force the authorities and higher-level management to respect their rights and claim their wages. But nowhere, such unions are recognized to a proper level, nor they are allowed to exercise their rights. This needs to change and major focus should be put on such elements of trade because Trade Unions are a very essential part of the Industrial Sector and play a very important role in both enhancing and diminishing the economy of a particular nation.

CHAPTER TWO

Introduction

A Trade Union in simple terms and general understating is nothing but a formal organization formed by the workers of a particular trade and industry who have together and with the consent of all of them in the union banned themselves from working for the management with an intention or common aim such as the protection of their integrity in the industry, demanding for higher pay wages, increasing the number of employees in the workplace and for better working conditions. It is a union formed by the workers which relate its intentions to the workplace and the management under which they work. These unions mainly work for the relationship between the employee and the employer.

The Trade Unions are regulated, monitored, and operated by a statute called The Trade Union Act, 1926 and this legislation defines the term Trade Unions which is as follows: "A combination, whether temporary or permanent, formed primarily to regulate the relations between workmen and employers or between workmen and workmen, or between employers and employers, or for imposing a restrictive condition on the conduct of any trade or business and includes any federation of two or more trade unions.[1]

The Trade Unions hold three major aims in its formation wherein workmen willingly demand 'Representation', 'Negotiation (Collective Bargaining)[2]', and 'Voice in a decision affecting workers like retrenchment and lay-off. The major challenge of any Trade Union is its recognition which means recognition by any employer of these unions for collective bargaining. The recognition takes place for the registered Trade Unions. The recognition of such Trade Unions is possible and can be made only by the employer and depends on his discretion.

The recognized Trade Unions get certain rights which they can legally and freely exercise under the regulation of the Trade Unions Actand these rights are meant for every member of the Trade Union and are legality under the ambit of Labor and Industrial Laws and Industrial relations for all the employers and the associates of the employers to allow the Trade Unions to exercise such rights and no member of such union should be restricted from these rights nor any of the rights should be hampered by any means.

[1] "Trade Union" means any combination, whether temporary or permanent, formed primarily for the purpose of regulating the relations between workmen and employers or between workmen and workmen, or between employers and employers, or for imposing restrictive conditions on the conduct of any trade or business, and includes any federation of two or more Trade Unions: Provided that this Act shall not affect—

(i) any agreement between partners as to their own business.

(ii) any agreement between an employer and those employed by him as to such employment; or

(iii) any agreement in consideration of the sale of the goodwill of a business or of instruction in any profession, trade, or handicraft.

[2] Collective bargaining is a fundamental right. It is rooted in the ILO Constitution and reaffirmed as such in the 1998 ILO Declaration on Fundamental Principles and Rights at Work. Collective bargaining is a key means through which employers and their organizations and trade unions can establish fair wages and working conditions. It also provides the basis for sound labor relations. Typical issues on the bargaining agenda include wages, working time, training, occupational health and safety and equal treatment. The objective of these negotiations is to arrive at a collective agreement that regulates terms and conditions of employment. Collective agreements may also address the rights and responsibilities of the parties thus ensuring harmonious and productive industries and workplaces. Enhancing the inclusiveness of collective bargaining and collective agreements is a key means for reducing inequality and extending labor protection.

CHAPTER THREE

Statement of the problem

In recent times, the workmen or the employees adopt ways such as lockouts and strikes to fulfil their demands and such forceful ways are increasing day by day. The core reason behind this issue is the unrecognition of Trade Unions and the violation of the rights conferred on the recognized Trade Unions. A small revamp in the concerned legislations can help resolve such issues and increase employee satisfaction which can, in turn, increase trade and boost the economic growth of a country.

With increasing economic development, the trade mechanisms are becoming advanced and industrial relations are not that smooth.The Trade Unions are not well treated as they deserve to be and these forces us to find and analyze the loopholes present in this system of law.

RESEARCH OBJECTIVES

A.To find out and evaluate the problems and perspectives which comes in the pathway of the procedure of recognition of Trade Unions.

B. To analyze and suggest proper policies and procedures in the legislation which can ease the process of recognition and protect the rights of recognized Trade Unions.

RESEARCH QUESTIONS

I.   What are the key threats to the rights of recognized Trade Unions?
II. What can be done to make the recognition of the unions better and the employers conferred with certain compulsions?

HYPOTHESIS

The clear point is that the Trade Unions which are an essential element of Trade, and Industrial Relations under the Labor and Industrial Laws are not well recognized in its sector and there should be an authority that can mandate the employers to provide such recognition to the Trade Unions.

Another thing is that the rights of the recognized unions should be highly protected from any sort of violation in the industry either by the employers or the employees.

SURVEY OF LITERATURE

The Trade Unions recognition and their rights are on a slopy surface and there is an urgent need of revamping the laws and regulations. The research carried out here has a major literature part which has been reviewed."The Law of Industrial Action and Trade Union Recognition"by 'John Bowers QC', 'Michael Duggan QC', 'David Reade QC', and 'Katherine Apps' is a book which elaborates the required reforms and new policies which must be adopted for the recognition of Trade Unions and the protection of the rights of those Trade Unions. Also, "A Critical Analysis of the Trade Union Recognition (Central) Rules 2021" by 'K.R. ShyamSundar' is a good source to the topic which mainly highlights the importance of Trade Union recognition and provides the latest framed rules by the government. Also, the article titled "Proposed Amendment on Recognition of Trade Unions – Trade Union (Amendment) Bill, 2018"published by MONDAQ in their magazineis also a very good literature material for the topic which deals with the majorly required amendments for the recognition of Trade Unions. "Mandatory Recognition of Trade Unions"authored by 'Somesh Jha' published by Business Standard, and"Rights of Trade Unions in India"by 'Shoronya Banerjee'published by iPleaders and "Proposed Developments in India's Law on Labor Unions"authored by 'VikramShroff'and 'Archita Mohapatra'published by The National Law Review. These articles and journal articles enlisted here play a very important role in providing further clarity to the topic.

METHODOLOGY ADOPTED

The present Research Paper is mainly 'Analytical' in nature with some 'Explanatory' aspects. The findings have been segregated into different chapters and each chapter consists of different sub-topics explaining and analyzing different concepts related to the topic this work revolves around.

SCOPE AND LIMITATIONS OF THE STUDY

The scope of this research work extends to the analysis of the core reasons for the non-recognition of the trade unions and how important it is for economic and industrial growth. The research has been limited to the already existing legislation and which includes provisions from different statutes and the proposed reports from different committees.

CHAPTER FOUR

Recognition and Registration of Trade Unions

Any Trade Union in the Industrial sector is not granted any sort of specific right when it comes to its recognition. But still, it has become essential and crucial in the country of India to develop and establish a specific mechanism wherein the trade union should be formally recognized by the employer. When it comes to the elaboration of this process, it is important to understand what is and when can a trade union be called a recognized one. Recognition of trade unions is a procedure by the employer of a workplace or industrial institute accepts the existence of a trade union and accepts it of having a representative trait and allows them to get involved and engage themselves in the discussions of such unions wherein the discussions are regarding the interests of the workers. Recognition is essential because it helps in the process of smooth collective bargaining and maintains stability in industrial relations. Another important step to be carried out here which has its vested benefits is the Registration of trade unions.

A trade union that is registered is assumed to be a corporate body and it has a legal entity and can inter alia enter contracts, acquire a property, and can sue others. Another major benefit of a registered trade union is that it gets protection from all kinds of criminal and civil liability and proceedings and certain contractual obligations. But it must be noted that the registration of trade unions is an optional step and not mandatory in anyways.

In general scenarios, it does not convey that if a trade union is registered under the Trade Unions Act, it does not imply automatically that the registered trade union gets a status of recognition from the employer. This can happen only if the states of India have specific legal provisions relating to the recognition of trade unions, but generally, as of now it is carried out and is mainly a matter of agreement between the trade union being recognized and their concerned employer. Impeccably, a trade union becomes legitimate through registration under the TU Act and after this process, that trade union can ask for recognition separately as a single bargaining agent either under the appropriate law or through an employee-employer agreement.

CHAPTER FIVE

Need for Recognition of Trade Unions

When one talks about the relationship between employee and the employer, 'Collective Bargaining' is the most important aspect which is discussed extensively and commonly. It must be noted that this right of collective bargaining is an essential right for all the trade unions but sadly this right is not provided to all the trade unions and is limited to only the recognized trade unions. Registration of trade unions is a separate thing totally and the recognition of trade unions as a sole bargaining agent with an intention of collective bargaining is a different and separate thing. Out of so many industrial strikes, most of them broke out on the question and issues relating to the recognition of the trade unions.

In general,industrial practices when carried out, the management/the employer allows collective bargaining and negotiations only from those trade unions which are recognized. It can be said that the recognition in terms of trade unions acts as a backbone of such unions for collective bargaining. The recognition of trade unions has always been the most debatable topic when it comes to labor and industrial laws and the sole reason behind this is that still and so far, there is no statute or central legislation on this topic or subject of "Recognition of Trade Unions."

In the judicial decision of Kalindi and Ors. V. Tata Locomotive and Engineering Co. Ltd[1], the Hon'ble Supreme Court of India had held that "There is no right to representation as such unless the company, by its standing orders, recognizes such rights. This decision of SC was reprised in the case of Bharat Petroleum Corporation Ltd. V. Maharashtra General. Kamgar Union &Ors.[2]

[1]Kalindi and Ors. V. Tata Locomotive and Engineering Co. Ltd AIR 914, 1960 SCR (3) 407

[2]Bharat Petroleum Corporation Ltd. V. Maharashtra General.Kamgar Union &Ors. AIR 1999 SC 401

CHAPTER SIX

Methods of Trade Union Recognition

The Recognition of Trade Unions is not a simple procedure, and the parties need to be followingcertain criteria. The Ministry of employment and labor had prepared their views which were based on the Tripartite System and based on their views certain drafts and bills were prepared to annotate the criteria which must be followed for the recognition and registration of the trade unions. (a) Firstly, only the 10% of the workers or s total of 100 workers numerically whichever is least will be considered as a union instead of any seven workers together, (b) Secondly, all the unions which are based on caste, craft, and category will neither be recognized nor be registered. (c) Thirdly, the law will be authoritative and will provide legality for the recognition of the trade unions and unions that are unrecognized will not be having any rights as such. [1]

These drafts and bills on three major occasions came up and showed before the government of the country but unfortunately, the day fell before these drafts could be discussed and thus, they could never take the form of an Act or Statute.

There was a major outburst that screamed the need for state intervention for trade unions recognitions. This was because the concerned employers wanted terms and conditions settlement of the work on the doctrine of 'Freedom of Contract.' The twist here was that this doctrine would be valid and will have a meaning only in that situation when both the parties to that contract are in a similar position to make their participation in the contract. The core reason behind this condition of this doctrine's performance is that if in any situation the parties to the contract are not placed in the same position similarly, the advantage of one party will make the other party suffer due to initial disadvantage and this doctrine will not work justly for the weaker party.

Before the independence, when Bombay Province observed such difficulties, they enacted legislation called "Bombay Industrial Relations Act" and later many states post-independence formulated provisions relating to the recognition of trade unions. The trade unions recognition can either be voluntary or statutory.[2]

Basic methods for the recognition of trade unions are as follows:

a. **Election by Secret Ballot:** Under this method of trade recognition a ballot system is followed. All the workers of a particular establishment who areeligible make a vote for the union they have chosen, and elections are conducted by an appointed neutral agent. This neutral agent is generally the Registrar of Unions and carries out the elections similar to general elections. Once this election is held, it has its validity for a certain time duration which is generally a minimum of two years. In the decision of **Food Corporation of India Staff Union V. Food Corporation of India and Ors.** theHon'ble Supreme Court of India, had elaborated certain procedures and norms which has to be followed while assessing the <u>assessing character</u> of the trade unions examined by the system of 'Secret Ballot.'

b. **Recognition by Management:** As classified above into two categories, this method is <u>Voluntary Recognition.</u> A successful trade union has an effective role in collective bargaining. The success and failure of collective bargaining depend on the willingness of the employer to recognize the union.

a. **The check-off Method:** In this method,every individual workergives authority to the management to deduct the fees of the union from his wages and request them to credit that fee to the chosen union. Doing this, the management becomes aware of the strengths of the unions which is evident to them. But the working system of any industrial workplace is risky to manipulation. This can mainly lead to a collision between the union the workers are favouring and the management. In this method, there may be situations when a genuine mistake may occur especially when the workers are in huge number. And apart from this, it also depends on the trade unions whether they accept this method and cooperate in its implementation.

d. **Verification of the Union Membership:** This method is carried out by the directorate of labor and is also adopted and used by various establishments as it was the resolution passed in a session held by the ILC. To make a start of this method, a particular procedure is required to be followed which begins when the management and the unions of a particular industry or an organization make an invitation to the labor directorate. The next step involves the responsibilities of the directorate himself wherein he collects all the relevant particulars and properties of the unions being recognized as they are necessary for the membership and registration of those unions. It is also the responsibility of this directorate to cross-check the unions and their particulars for duplicate membership for which the fees book, claims lists, account books, and membership records of the unions are closely and deeply scrutinized. The dual membership of any trade union is strictly not allowed. In the final step of this method, the directorate prepares a final and verified list for the unions, employers, and the purpose of the government as well but only after thoroughly and double-checking physical sampling and records of all the workers which is a mandatory step in the situation of duplication or doubt. But even after such well-elaborated steps and rules, this method of trade union recognition cannot be considered reliable especially when the concerned establishment is a large one and is highly dynamic which means that it can change in very short intervals.

It is evident that similarly in the case of a corporate body or a company, a Memorandum of Association is required; a Memorandum of Agreement is also required when an employer accepts or agrees to recognize a particular trade union. In general cases, any trade union can also write an application to the industrial court if they want to get recognition and if that trade union satisfies and fulfils all the necessary and required conditions of that labour court including the compliance with the provisions of the Act, then the court issues a recognition certificate to that union. Amongst all of these widespread methods of trade recognition, the method which is rapidly growing in the industrial sector is the 'Secret Ballot System.' It took its hike when the Hon'ble Supreme Court mandated this procedure when it made an order for a secret ballot in the case of **Food Corporation. [3]**

[1] http://www.delhi.gov.in/wps/wcm/connect/doit_labour/Labour/ Home/Acts Implemented/Details of the Acts Implemented/The Trade Unions Act, 1926/accesses30/07/2016

G.M.Kothari ,A Study On Industrial Law,Wadhwa And Company, Nagpur,5THEdition,2002,pg no.316 G.M.Kothari ,A Study On Industrial Law,Wadhwa And Company, Nagpur,5THEdition/2002,,pg no 325

[2] H L Kumar, 'Labor Problems and remedies', Universal Law Publication Co: New Delhi, ninth edition 2010 p. 297

Needs and rights of recognized trade union, SmithiChand

AIR 1960 SC 914

AIR 1999 SC 401

[3] Food Corporation of India Staff v. Food Corporation of India AndOrs. on 17 February 1995

CHAPTER SEVEN

Reports, Statutes, and Trade Unions Recognition

Historically speaking, the legislation relating to labor in India was at a slow pace in its developing stage. The time flew by likea bullet and the development stage of industrial relations laws reached the peak of its development only during World War I. This was the time when numerous strikes were broken out between the factory workers and the industrial workers. The time and mechanisms favored the workers of both types, and a majority of these strikes were highly successful whichled to the ILO getting established and this action heavily paved the path for the 'Trade Union Movement' in the country of India.

A suit was filed by **Binny& Co. Ltd.** against the **Textile Labor Union[1]**and in the year 1920, the High Court of Madras in which the court granted an injunction and restrained the officials of the union from inducing the workers to break their employment contracts. This was done when the workers refused to return to their work which was a result of the leader who used to regulate the activities related to trade and this made the trade unions feel the necessity of legislative protection. A resolution was successfully moved in the Central Legislative Assembly in the year 1921 by N.M. Joshi who was the Generals Secretary of all India Trade Union Congress and this resolution sought and demanded an introduction and formulation of certain legislations by the Government to protect the trade unions, and this move was strongly opposed and protested by the employers. The legislation of the Trade Unions Act was passed in the year 1926 and came into force and became operative on June1, 1927.

Even after such legislation for the trade unions, it was observed that there was no provision in this Act relating to the recognition of the trade unions and this followed up till 1947. Later an amendment was brought to the Trade Unions Act, 1929 and this amendment inserted certain provisions in Chapter III-A from Section 28A to 28I of the Act. Herein, Section 28A specifically dealt with the definition of the term "appropriate government", Section 28B dealt with the constitution, powers, appointment and the procedures of the labor court and the recognition of the trade unions was specifically dealt with from Section 28C to Section 28I. But the unfortunate move here was that since the day this provision got inserted into the Act, it did not come into force and still, it remains a dead letter. After this, there were several attempts made for the compulsory recognition of the trade unions in the years 1950, 1978, and 1988 but none of them could get a material form.

After reviewing, evaluating, and analyzing several differentlegislations relating to labor in 1969 and after reviewing the Trade Unions Act in 1929, the National Labor Commission proposed a list of recommendations which is as follows:[2]

a. The commission strongly recommended a Compulsory Registration of the Trade Unions.
b. It stated that if any trade union is not complying with the conditions of the filing of membership or the returns, effective measures must be taken for their cancellation.
c. It should be made compulsory for the Employers to recognize the Trade unions, and this should be made compulsory by the Central Legislation as the undertakings specified.
d. All the recognized trade unions must be provided with certain statutory rights which are exclusive.
e. These statutory exclusive rights should include rights and facilities such as entering into the agreements of collective bargaining, sole representation, inspection, check-off, holding of negotiations and discussions, etc.
f. The Commission lastly recommended that the minority unions should also be allowed to represent their workers in the redressal relating to the individual grievances such as discharge, dismissal, etc.

[1]Binny& Co. Ltd. v. Textile Labor Union1996 87 CompCas 438 Mad, 1995 (1) CTC 73, (1995) ILLJ 588 Mad
[2] The redefinition of labor regulation largely along bipartite lines was an overt aim in the proceedings of the SNCL when it was eventually

set up in 1999: "consistent with the spirit of the new context, and of interdependence is to settle disputes through bilateral discussions
and negotiations. All efforts must be made to promote bilateralism based on mutual interests and universally accepted rights" Report of
SNCL p. 310. 3The Chairman took recourse to Indian philosophic thought in explaining how conflicting positions would be reconciled: "it would usually be possible to resolve that conflict, provided we take recourse to two principles which are known to Indian culture for ages These principles
are very simple: one principle is Sameeksha — You try to discriminate dispassionately between the pros and cons of both the competing
concepts The other principle is Saman way, synthesis I do not think that there is any problem which we may have to face during the course
of our elaborate deliberations, which may ultimately defy our determined effort to find a rational solution to it. Rational or harmonious
synthesis, attempting to resolve the conflict between the two competing ideas would be possible provided wemakean earnest and
determined effort to try to eliminate our personal affiliations and meet the challenge of the problem in an objective manner", p. A8(Appendix
III). 4Ibid; pp.1. 5The terms of reference are noted as:
(1) To review the changes in conditions of labor since Independence and to report on existing conditions of labor.

(2) To review the existing legislative and other provisions intended to protect the interests of labor, to assess their working and to advise how far these
provisions serve to implement the Directive Principles of State Policy in the Constitution on labor matters and the national objectives of
establishing a socialist society and achieving planned economic development;
(3) To study and report in particular on—
(i) the levels of workers' earnings, the provisions relating to wages, the need for fixation of minimum wages including a national minimum
wage, the means of increasing productivity, including the provision of incentives to workers;
(ii) the standard of living and the health, efficiency, safety, welfare, housing, training and education of workers and the existing arrangements for administration of labor welfare— both at the Centre and in the States;
(iii) the existing arrangements for social security;
(iv) the state of relations between employers and workers and the role of

trade unions and employers' organizations in promoting healthyindustrial relations and the interests of the nation.

CHAPTER EIGHT

Rights of Recognized Trade Unions and their Legal Status

When a trade union gets recognized by the employer it becomes a corporate body with a common seal and perpetual succession. Its legal status is binding and operative just as a corporate body and it becomes a legal entity just like a company or a firm. A trade union that is recognized becomes capable of acquiring, holding, transferring, or selling any immovable or movable property and can enter into contracts or become a party to a contract. Like the legal status of any corporate body, a recognized trade union can sue and be sued in its name. Also, under certain specified conditions, no legal proceeding or a civil suit can be filed or initiated against any registered trade union concerning any activity associated with a trade dispute.

Apart from such major aspects of the attained legal status, a trade union once recognized is provided with certain statutory rights which are exclusive. The trade unions consist of office-bearers and these office-bearers after the recognition of the concerned trade union gets the authority to collect the payable sums by the members to their union on the premises where the wages are paid to them. These unions get a right to put up notices on the noticeboard of the premises of the undertaking in which their workers are employed and they can also affix the notice thereon. The trade unions after being recognized get the right and authority to hold and organize certain activities for their workers such as they become authorized to hold discussions for the concerned employees. These concerned employees are those members of the union who are not allowed to interfere with the due working of the undertaking. These unions can meet with the employer or any of the representatives of the employer or any person appointed by that employer on his behalf to discuss the grievances of the employees working in his undertaking. [1]

Such trade unions, in necessary situations also have rights to inspect any place of the undertaking in which their workers are employed with a purpose to prevent and settle any industrial dispute. When any domestic or departmental enquiry is held by the employer, the recognized trade unions have the right to appear in such enquiry on behalf of any of its employees. Finally, and majorly, a recognized trade union solely has the right to appoint nominees or themselves who can represent their workmen on the Works Committee which is constituted under Section 3 of the Central Act.

[1]Incorporation of registered Trade Unions. —Every registered Trade Union shall be a corporate by the name under which it is registered and shall have perpetual succession and a body common seal with power to acquire and hold bothmovable and immovable property and to contract and shall by the said name sue and be sued.

CHAPTER NINE

Advantages of Trade Union Recognition

Once a Trade Union gets recognized, it gets vested with certain advantages which helps its workers and in its operation in the long run. It has been observed that various employers prefer dealing directly with the concerned workers or their elected representatives without the involvement of any trade union, but they must understand that working closely with the recognized trade unions sprinkles various advantages which can help in an easy and smooth operative procedure for all the labor and industrial related activities.

Certain advantages of trade union recognition are:

a. The recognition of a trade union establishes a <u>Single Point of Contract</u> and when there is a single body for carrying out the negotiation procedure of terms and conditions for the workers of that union, such process is simpler and easier than dealing with each worker on an individual basis. A point to note here is that in this collective style of negotiating, certain information needs to be disclosed for collective bargaining.

b. More <u>Work Involvement</u> comes in after recognition of a trade union. As the terms and conditions are negotiated and issues of the workplace are consulted with a recognized trade union, the workers of the union will feel more of their involvement in the running of a business. Through this, the employer can encourage and trust the workforce of his organization and the workers will help in improving the retention rates.

c. The <u>Experience of Employment Relations</u> becomes better as the trade unions have a broad perspective on the issues affecting the organization. The representatives of the union have experience in employment relations which is useful and act as a good source of legal and good practice advice on employment law issues and HR.

CHAPTER TEN

Conclusion & Suggestion

After a major evaluation, analysis, and assessment of legal pints and legislations relating to the recognition of trade unions and their rights, as a verdict, it can be clearly stated that there is no uniform law in the legislations formulated by the states and the government at both levels. Also, the amendment of the Central Act in 1947 is a waste and remains a dead law. It can be concluded that there is no smoothness and regulation in the process of trade union recognition and this process depends upon the discretion of the management or the employer and the victim which suffers here is the Trade Union which as a result loses its deserved rights.

It should be understood that the law of life is "Change." Law should be a dynamic element and cannot remain protected from such changes of the society and to be effective and just,it should comply with all the societal changes. When it comes to the concept of 'Labor', it has undergone various and different kinds of changes that are far beyond reach. The legislation relating to labor must undergo constant revisions on regular basis. It is an essential aspect of legislation and amendments to cope up with the changes and implementation to the society.

The importance and the value of Trade Unions have been growing gradually post-independence of our country. In the world of Industrial Relations and Labor Mechanisms, Collective Bargaining plays a very essential role, and it completely depends on the recognition of the Trade Unions. It has been noticed that the attitude of the legislature and the executive is very hostile and bogus towards the legislations after the enactment of the Trade Union Act, 1926 even after several scenarios where the consideration for trade union recognition came up. Thus, it is suggested that necessary and major steps must be taken to formulate proper and relevant legislations and to enforce the amendment which was brought out in 1947 which remains a dead letter.

www.ingramcontent.com/pod-product-compliance
Lightning Source LLC
Chambersburg PA
CBHW072145150726
48002CB00004B/1632